big
the musical

Project Manager: Sy Feldman
Cover Artwork: David Febland Studios, New York, New York

DAVID SHIRE (Music). Broadway: *Baby* (Tony nominations, Best Score and Musical); Off-Broadway: *Starting Here, Starting Now* (Grammy nomination), Closer Than Ever, (Outer Critic's Circle, Best Musical), incidental music for *The Loman Family Picnic, Shmulnik's Waltz, As You Like It* (NYSF). Film scores include *Norma Rae* (Academy Award, Best Song), *The Conversation, All the President's Men, Farewell My Lovely, Short Circuit, Return to Oz, Taking of Pelham 1-2-3, Saturday Night Fever* (two Grammy Awards). TV scores: (four Emmy Awards nominations) include "Raid on Entebbe," "Sarah Plain and Tall," "My Antonia," "Serving in Silence," "The Heidi Chronicles," "Alice." Recorded songs include Barbra Streisand's "What About Today?" and "Starting Here, Starting Now, " and "With You I'm Born Again." He is married to Didi Conn and has two sons, Matthew 20, and Daniel, 3.

Photography: Paul McKibbins

RICHARD MALTBY, JR. (*lyrics*) co-wrote the lyrics for *Miss Saigon* which is currently running on Broadway, and in five international productions. He directed and conceived *Ain't Misbehavin'* (Tony Award as Best Director, Best Musical). He directed Andrew Lloyd Webber's *Song & Dance* on Broadway (Tony Award for its star Bernadette Peters). With composer David Shire he wrote and directed *Starting Here, Starting Now* (RCA album nominated for a Grammy), *Baby* (nominated for seven Tony Awards) and *Closer Than Ever* (Outer Critic's Circle awards for best score and best musical). The son of the well-known orchestra leader, Mr. Maltby also contributes devilish crossword puzzles to *Harper's* magazine He is married to Janet Brenner and has five children: Nicholas, 28; David, 27; Jordan, 7; Emily, 5; and Charlotte, 2.

I Want to Go Home

Lyrics by
RICHARD MALTBY, Jr.

Music by
DAVID SHIRE

Moderately

This is ex - cit - ing. It's an ad - ven - ture. I get to see some things that most kids nev - er do. That guy just took a knife out of his

I Want to Go Home - 4 - 1
PF9635

4

6

Fun

Lyrics by
RICHARD MALTBY, Jr.

Music by
DAVID SHIRE

Fun - 5 - 1
PF9635

Stars, Stars, Stars

Lyrics by
RICHARD MALTBY, Jr.

Music by
DAVID SHIRE

Moderate (in one)

Stars,
(2nd time instrumental)
I can give you stars. A hun-dred bil - lion stars in the sky. We can watch them float by.

Stars, Stars, Stars - 3 - 1
PF9635

Cross the Line

Lyrics by
RICHARD MALTBY, Jr.

Music by
DAVID SHIRE

Moderately, "Philly-shuffle"

This is our dance,_ got - ta come dance with me.
You can dance, too,_ got - ta come try it now.

This is our chance,_ got - ta move in - stant - ly.
Do what I do,_ fake_ if you don't know how.

An - y min - ute now, it's gon - na have flown a - way.
An - y - thing the kids are do - in' 'll be o - kay.

Cross the Line - 9 - 1
PF9635

22

Dancing All the Time

Lyrics by
RICHARD MALTBY, Jr.

Music by
DAVID SHIRE

How'd that lit - tle girl slip_ by?_____ How'd that stream of dreams run_

dry? Some-where in my teens I__ seemed to lose the means to_ fly._

My!

What I'd give to_ be laugh - ing all the time,_____ to be
laugh - ing all the time._____ And I'm

Lyrics by
RICHARD MALTBY, Jr.

Stop, Time

Music by
DAVID SHIRE

Stop, Time - 3 - 1
PF9635

I Want to Know

Lyrics by
RICHARD MALTBY, Jr.

Music by
DAVID SHIRE

I Want to Know - 5 - 1
PF9635

34

I Want to Know - 5 - 4
PF9635

Coffee, Black!

Lyrics by
RICHARD MALTBY, Jr.

Music by
DAVID SHIRE

Golly, you're cute this morn-ing,—

Coffee, Black! - 4 - 4
PF9635

One Special Man

Lyrics by
RICHARD MALTBY, Jr.

Music by
DAVID SHIRE

It's awe-some, a- maz-ing, it's hard to be - lieve, the se - cret, the cos - mos had

One Special Man - 5 - 1
PF9635